LETTING GO IS AN ACQUIRED TASTE

CHRISTINA HART

LETTING GO IS AN ACQUIRED TASTE

ISBN-13: 978-1539177104
ISBN-10: 1539177106

For the few men I've loved –
I'm letting you go now.

THE ART OF LETTING GO

The art of letting go
and moving on
is an acquired taste
one only knows after
they know
nothing else
for long enough.
The first step is forced,
and

   every

     step

       after

         is felt.

LET THEM LEAVE

I traced a circle
around the beauty mark
on my thigh,
marking what was still mine.
Some things they can
never take with them,
so if they want to leave,
let them.

I LISTENED

For years I had been
holding on to men
who no longer wished
to hold on to me.
So I listened.
I let them go.

HURRICANE NIGHTS

I was holding on
to hurricane nights
and lit candles
and my acoustic guitar
resting in your hands.
I was holding on
to the sound of
your voice saying my name
and the peace I felt
with your arms
around me.
I was holding on
to documentaries in bed
and your beautiful eyes
closed as you sang
Rocket Man and all
the songs we never finished.
I was holding on
to our first text and
last phone call and
the plane ticket you
offered but never sent.
I was holding on
to our first Christmas
together
and the last few Christmas Eves
apart
and I've been thinking

We should be together.
We should be kissing
even if there
isn't any mistletoe
because if I have you
there's reason to celebrate and
fuck, your lips were mine.
They were always supposed
to be mine.
I was holding on
to hope and banana pancakes
on Sundays.
I was holding on
to Main Street and
sunsets in Jersey.
I was holding on
to two streets that
separated us and
blizzards that couldn't
keep us apart.
I was holding on
to you.
I was holding on
to us.
And it was killing me.

ALL OUR SONGS

And all our songs
are now just
songs
that
remind
me
of
you.

DIGGING GRAVES

One can only dig
their own grave
for so long.
Eventually you hit
bottom
and decide
whether you want to
get in
now
or
later.

SOMETIMES IT IS
JUST THAT SIMPLE

To sum it all up,
he taught me
two things:

I am still not
good enough,

and I am too
good for him.

THE BURN

I burned my finger
on the stovetop yesterday
and even though I am
28 years old
I am *still* learning
that some things
are too hot to touch.
I am tired of
feeling the burn.
And I am beginning
to learn that
sometimes
it is better
to
      walk

          away.

I WAS NEVER A WIFE

I could never see myself
as a wife
but they could.
Or at least
they said they could.
I lost count of
the men
who said they
wanted to
marry me one day,
after the first one
packed those wishes and
left.
He's married now,
to a beautiful girl
with blue eyes
and
everything
he never saw in me.

SHATTERING HEARTS

One day
I will shatter hearts
with all the stones
they threw at me.

WORDS LIKE KNIVES

I took back my heart and
crammed it into my bag
and walked away for the
third time,
the fourth time
(who's counting?),
the last time.
I promised myself I'd
never let myself fall
for green eyes and
beautiful lies and
words that felt
like knives
ever
again.

STAR-STAINED

I almost forgot how pretty
the darkness was.
My star-stained eyes
had grown too
used to it all
to notice
anything else was
actually out there.

*(Beyond this and you
and all the promises
I was still waiting
for you to keep.)*

TOMB

You were true love and
worshipping hands and
gratitude in your eyes.
You were birthday cards
and presents and surprises
to make me smile.
They were filthy words
and empty beds and
lies that sliced my insides.
They could
never love me like
you did and
they never tried.
My body has become
a tomb and I am learning
how to unfeel all the
hands that touched me
that were not yours.

SAVE A SPOT FOR ME

Sometimes I still
see you in strangers
and I hope your
eyes aren't as
loveless
as theirs are.
I hope your
dreams have
built a home
from your bones
and I hope
it's cozy and
unsettling
all at the
same time
because
for some reason
you are still
saving a spot
for me.

IT'S SO MUCH EASIER BEING ALONE

It's so much easier
being
alone.
I know the ways
I can hurt me.

SHADES OF BLUE

I turned too many
shades of blue
choking on all the things
I wanted to say to you.
"I thought this was real"
must have gone down
wrong and
"Come back to me"
was lost somewhere
in my windpipe.
Do not resuscitate
and do not bring
flowers to my grave.
Let the beauty be
before the death
of it all.
Let it be in knowing
what we had and
what we could
have had again
had one or both
of us not been
so god damn
stubborn.

THEY JUST DON'T WANT TO HEAR IT

There are only so many
ways you can tell someone
you love them
until it finally
sinks in
that they just
don't
want
to
hear
it.

I AM FORGETTING

I am forgetting the sound
of your voice.
I love you.
I am forgetting the sound
of your voice.
I need you.
I am forgetting the sound
of your voice.
I miss you.
I am trying to remember
the sound of your voice
and it still hurts
but not in the same way
it used to.

WINDOW SHOPPING

I am window shopping
in the faces of men,
looking for something
resembling love
and I do not see it
anywhere.
What a tragedy.

MAD

You are either
mad
or
you are not.
Love only
infuriates it.

BURN THEM, IT'S EASIER

I light torches
at the feet of
men who say
they want me.
They all sound
the same at this point
and I can no longer
distinguish the
truth from the lies.
For once, words aren't enough.
I need someone to prove it.

PASSING NOTES

I'm passing notes
in class again
to the girl
who used to be me.
Leave him
before he leaves you.
He isn't worth it.
You are worth
so much more
than 2am texts
and conversations
he will never remember.

I STILL FEEL IT

I can still feel
the way you
held my hand
and told me
it would all
be okay.
It wasn't.
I can still taste
the sting of
the last time
you told me
this love was
forever.
It wasn't.
I can still picture
your eyes
looking at your
phone as you
told me it was no one.
It wasn't.
I can still hear
your voice
telling me
I was e v e r y t h i n g
to you.
I wasn't.
I can still hear
the banging of

the drums
in my heart
as I told you
I was done
this time
and you thought
I was joking.
I wasn't.

SEEING RED

Red lips and
stiff drinks.
Do you want to watch her dance?
Bras matching
underwear and
thongs and
glittery stages.
Would you ever be with another woman?
Dollar bills and men
on coke and a lock on
the women's bathroom door.
Let me walk you there.
Let me make sure you're safe.
Neon lights and makeup
and legs that went on for days
and you put your hand
on my thigh.
You're so beautiful, baby.
True colors and liars and
hustlers and all the things
that are not me.
Could you ever see yourself
having a threesome?
Back doors and parking lots
and people escaping
one thing or another that
they fucking hate.
I love you.

I can still hear it.
I can still hear it.
I can still hear it.
This isn't love.
This isn't love
and I want nothing
that looks anything
like it.
I want nothing
like the red lips
and sugary hips
and dances
meant to seduce.
I want nothing
like the men
tossing dollar bills
onto the stage
and slipping them
into bra cups over
women's breasts
and into the strings
of their underwear.
Do you think she's pretty?
I think she's pretty
but I do not think
watching you flirt
with the pretty stripper
turns me on and
I do not think
any of these things
are impressive and I
do not think I will give up

the sunset on a cool evening
for a show like this
on a flashing stage
with women whose eyes
are even emptier than mine.

TRAIN WRECK

This was
nothing short
of a train wreck
that ran off the
tracks two stops
away from
nowhere.
I just got off
before you did.

REGRETS LIKE VULTURES

Our regrets swept upon us
like vultures, picking at the
things we wished we'd done and
the things we wished we hadn't.
Life is little more than
a heartbeat away from
getting things right
the first time and
a lifetime spent
wishing that we had.

TEENAGE BLUES

I remember sixteen.
I was wide-eyed and
fresh-faced and full of hope
and longing and curiosity.
Back then
I thought my
feelings were
so adult.
As an adult
I spent my time
searching for a love
to bring back those young
butterflies to kick my ass.
I wanted the butterflies.
I wanted the blues.
I wanted.
I wanted.
I wanted.
I received.
And I am still
recovering.

THE NOOSE

There were men.
Of course there
were men –
men like the noose
I chose to
cut myself from.

I AM STILL LEARNING

Promises always
tasted sweeter
coming from
the lips
of someone
who
would
never
keep
them.
There is beauty
in the challenge.
There is a bitter hurt
in the aftertaste.
I have learned.
I have learned.
I am still learning.
It was fun.
It was fun.
It is no longer fun.

REMEMBERING TO FORGET

Your grip on my wrist
and your hands in my hair.
I am trying to forget.
Your hands on my back
and my body, shaking,
beneath you.
I am trying to forget.
You tracing words on my skin
and my skin traced in your words.
I am trying to forget.
Your hands.
Your hands.
Your hands.
I am trying to forget.
Your mouth on mine and
the music that came from it.
I am trying to remember.
Your last goodbye and
the promise of our next hello.
I am trying to remember.
Your hands.
Your fucking hands and
mine, intertwined, locked at
the red light before we
crossed the street to go to
Quick Chek to grab coffee and
a sandwich.
I am trying to remember.

Your words. Your words.
Your words. You said so many words
and I am trying to remember them all
and I am trying not to forget them all
and I am trying to keep them locked
in this place in my chest that used to
keep my heart warm.
Do I still have a heart?
Do you have it?
Did you take it with you?
I am trying to remember.
You, in the kitchen,
making something healthy.
You, choking on broccoli.
Me, laughing about it.
You, being upset.
"I almost died!" you said.
We were fighting just
before you choked.
What were we fighting about?
I am trying to remember.
It was stupid. It was usually
stupid, the things we fought
about. The things we'd use to
get to each other to make
each other mad so we could
make up for it later that night.
The things we argued about
were so fucking stupid
and if you were here now
I would make you broccoli
and I would remind you

not to choke and you
would pretend you were irritated
and you would wrestle me on
the bed and make me shut up
and you would laugh and
I would laugh.
I need to forget.
I need to forget.
Your hands.
Your hands.
Your hands.
Your eyes.
Your mouth.
Your smile.
Your favorite sweatshirt.
Your healthy crap you loved.
Your magic.
Your laugh.
Fuck. I remember that.
I remember your laugh.
Your eyes.
I remember those, too.
Your smile.
I am trying to remember how
to try to forget.
Your hands are
probably holding on
to someone else's
right now and I am
trying not to think of
that because that will
kill me.

I am trying to forget.
I promise.
I am trying to forget.
Your lips the way they
formed that sentence.
"This is it. You and me. Always."
I am trying to forget.
I am trying to remember.
I am trying to remember
that you don't
want to talk to me anymore.
"You are the love of my life."
I am trying to forget that you said that.
I am trying to forget November.
I am trying to forget the years prior.
I am forgetting to remember to forget.
Love is too confusing
and I am confusing all
these men with you
and their eyes don't look
like yours
and their hands don't feel
like yours
and their voices don't sound
like yours
and their intentions are not pure
like yours.
I am trying to forget.
But I will always remember you.

I DON'T HEAR THE MUSIC ANYMORE

Somewhere
there's an empty hall
where all our songs
are playing.
We're supposed to
be dancing,
but I don't even
hear the music
anymore.

DEAR STRANGER

Dear Stranger,

You said less than fifteen words
to me and I forget none of them.
There was a story somewhere in
your smile that I wanted to read.
I have not felt desire in months but
I felt it for you somewhere in the
six inches of space you gave to me
until I finally forced myself to
look at you. I have never seen
someone take a white t-shirt and a
baseball cap and make it so fucking
memorable. I never understood
the romance in a three-minute
encounter with a person that
fate slid to you over a table and
dared you to bet on. I never
understood the remorse
of keeping your chips to yourself
in a single game that may have
changed everything. I never
understood the footsteps in the
dance that is asked of you when
a beautiful chance presents itself.
There was a kindness in your eyes
one may only recognize as hope.
And I recognized it.

And I fumbled over my words
that were probably stupid but
what I really should have said was
"You, you with the golden smile and
sincerity dripping from your eyes,
what is your name? Tell me it now
before I forget to ask. Tell me it now
before you are gone as quickly as
you came. Tell me it now so I might
find you again." But, I didn't say that.
I did forget to ask. And you were gone
as quickly as you came and now I look
for you in every gray car, underneath
every white t-shirt and baseball cap,
in every stranger I see.
I have not felt desire since
I shared those six inches of space
with you.
And I refuse to see this
romance as tragic because if there is
hope like the hope that was promised
to me in your eyes then I believe I
will find you again. If not in you, then
in someone who will take that chance
and grab it by the balls and
just
fucking
kiss
me
already
as we were meant to.
Our paths may have crossed and I

may have been changed by it but
I want it to mean more.
More than this regret
of never knowing
your name.
More than being sorry
I never asked.
More than being sorry you
never told me.
I want it to mean enough
to you to alter its course
and plant me in the winds
heading straight to you.
I want it to mean more.
I want it to mean forever or
something that at least
feels like it could have been.
Something that feels like
until now, all of the
somethings were just
nothings
waiting for us to happen.

Made in the USA
San Bernardino, CA
27 April 2018